. . . those who have gone . . . vanished.
Literally . . . something that is all used up.

Emil W. Haury, The Hohokam

HOHOKAM

Richard Shelton

With Hohokam pottery designs from photographs
by Steven Trubitt

sun lizard book number two

Tucson Arizona 1986

SUN/gemini Press

SUN/gemini Press, Inc.
Post Office Box 42170
Tucson, AZ 85733

Shelton, Richard
    Hohokam.

    (Sun lizard book; no. 2)
        1. Hohokam culture--Poetry.   I. Title.
II. Series.
PS3569.H39367H6   1986   811'.54   86-968
ISBN 0-933313-04-7
ISBN 0-933313-05-5 (pbk.)

The pottery sherds are from Snaketown, Arizona, Site AZ
U:13:1 (ASM). Epigraph page, figures A, B, C, D, F, H, I, J,
K, M, N, O, P, and colophon page are Santa Cruz Red-on-
buff, Colonial Period, 700-900 A.D. Endsheets, title page,
and figures E & G are Sacaton Red-on-buff, Sedentary
Period, 900-1000 A.D.

Books/Chapbooks by RS

JOURNAL OF RETURN, Kayak Press, 1969
THE TATTOOED DESERT, University of Pittsburgh Press, 1971
OF ALL THE DIRTY WORDS, University of Pittsburgh Press, 1972
THE HEROES OF OUR TIME, Best Cellar Press, 1972
CALENDAR, Baleen Press, 1972
AMONG THE STONES, Monument Press, 1973
YOU CAN'T HAVE EVERYTHING, University of Pittsburgh Press, 1975
CHOSEN PLACE, Best Cellar Press, 1975
THE BUS TO VERACRUZ, University of Pittsburgh Press, 1978
DESERT WATER, Monument Press, 1981
SELECTED POEMS: 1969–1981, University of Pittsburgh Press, 1982
A KIND OF GLORY, Copper Canyon Press, 1982

Of the small press books listed, only two are in print. Inquiries should be addressed as follows:

CALENDAR:
Richard Shelton
1548 North Plaza de Lirios
Tucson, AZ 85745

A KIND OF GLORY:
Copper Canyon Press
P.O. Box 271
Port Townsend, WA 98368

Forthcoming, 1986/87, THE OTHER SIDE OF THE STORY (Prose).
Inquiries to:
Confluence Press
Spaulding Hall
Lewis-Clark State College
Lewiston, ID 83501

One

In a lost century before white men came,
bringing with them history and time,
rivers ran through the desert
deep and brown after late-summer rains,
swift and clear in spring.
Even then, in a lost century,
a prehistoric time, the young were young.

It is spring in the desert. A girl
walks down a path through tall
arrowweeds beside a riverbed.
We see her from a great distance,
from beyond a chasm history cannot bridge,
but even from this distance she is beautiful.
She pauses, looking ahead and listening
as if she expects to hear someone coming
toward her on the path. She is wearing
sandals of yucca fiber, a narrow
cotton apron, a bracelet of bone
carved in the shape of a snake
and on a leather thong around her neck
a small clamshell whose inner surface
is inlaid with tiny squares of turquoise.
Her hair is long and dark.

The river is broad this time of year
but shallow. She kneels to drink,
making the customary sign of thanks
to the river which has always provided
water for the corn and for the people
since before anyone can remember.
Her father has told her it was so
in the time of his father's father.
As she rises, she looks across the river
at three small gray mountains,
cone-shaped peaks, isolated
on a flat desert floor. The Three Sisters.
They are old, worn down. She knows
their story. Each refused a husband;
now each must lean upon the others
under a cruel sun and stagger on
toward the river none of them will reach.

A young man is coming toward her
on the twisting path. She hears him
before she can see him and turns aside
into a little bower in the arrowweeds
near the bank of the river. He will be
naked except for sandals, and powerfully
built, with strong arms and shoulders.
He will be carrying a stone hoe
lashed to a haft of ironwood,
and humming a tuneless chant
in time to the rhythm of his walking.

As he passes, she makes a mocking
gesture with her hand and laughs
a word of derision. The word is lost
to us, as is her name and the chant
he is humming; but a ritual has begun
which will lead to ceremony, children,
much labor and pain. She is learning
to make pottery and knows she is pleasing
to his eyes. He is a farming man.
She excites him more than a stand
of healthy corn rustling in the wind.

c

Two

They taunt one another at first.
He teases her because her fingers
are stained red from the dye
she uses for patterns on her pottery.
She becomes proud and says her father
is a hunter. She cannot stay here
talking to the son of a farmer;
it would bring shame to her father.
She has come to gather arrowweeds to repair
the house. She must get them and be gone.
She has no time to talk to a farmer's son.

He grabs a handful of her hair
and says it is too long and thick.
It should be cut and used for rope
or something, as her mother's is.
It is no use except to hide her breasts,
which are no use either, since she
has no husband to give her children.
She is a useless girl with long hair,
small breasts and no husband. Her father
is a vain man who cannot feed his family
nearly as well as a farmer can.

d

He lets go of her hair. She laughs again
and says that when summer comes
her mother will help her cut her hair
and braid sandal straps for the hunters.
Her mother is gentle when cutting hair.
What need is there for a rough husband
to do what a mother does better?
There is a strong young hunter . . .
who needs new sandals. Her father
has favored him in all things. Perhaps
she will have a husband by summer.

He reaches out to touch her breast
and his hand brushes across the shell
hanging from her neck. He pulls his hand
back as if it had been burned.
She turns away quickly, hunches
her shoulders and clutches the amulet
in both hands. They are quiet a moment,
remembering the law of all the clans:
Any man who takes the shell of virginity
by force will be put to death. It can
be claimed if the girl has willingly lain
with the man, but otherwise must be given
by the girl who wears it or her parents.

She turns back to him and places
his hand on her breast, carefully
so it will not touch the shell.
She smiles. Then her hair covers his face.
He cannot see, but he takes
one dark, young nipple in his mouth
like a hungry baby. She closes her eyes.

Three

Later he will present his prize
to her father, the shell of turquoise
which she tore from her neck and offered
to him before they made love.
He will promise her father a large
supply of corn at the next harvest.
There will be intricate ceremonies.
Her mother will grumble about a hunter's
daughter taking as a husband
the son of a farmer. It will mean
learning the ways of a different clan.
Her father's clan is better
and more powerful. How can the daughter
of a hunter consider such a thing.

Her mother will go on and on.
But the girl will go to live
with the farmers. She will learn to build
canals for irrigation and to terrace
the slopes along the river with stones.
She will learn to use a sharp stick
to dig up the desert soil and plant corn,
and she will learn to use a stone hoe
until her delicate potter's hands are raw,
and then she will learn to make pottery
according to the clan's designs.
And she will learn to have many children,
hoping each one will be a son.

e

Four

By the time her cropped hair is gray
she will have had twelve children, five
of whom have lived, and three of them
are sons, strong farmer's sons.
She is proud. When the crops are bad
she saves her children extra food
from that portion owed to the hunters
in return for the meat they provide.
She does not fear the penalties;
the hunters bring in little meat
and her children are young and need food.

She knows how hard life is for a farmer
in a dry land. She has made
corn grow where even her husband
said it could not be grown. She has
watched the old fields dying
and worked with the men digging
a canal to bring water from the river
to the new fields. She has sacrificed
at the time of the new moon
and scattered pollen at dawn
in the four sacred directions
and, secretly, upon the river to please
the god who lives there. Her pottery
is much in demand. Let the hunters
have pots in return for the corn
she owes them. She and her family
have grown the corn. They will keep
enough to feed their children.

*The hunters complain that her husband
is cheating them, but she can
threaten a man with a fishing spear
if one chooses to complain to her,
as several have. Her voice is low
and harsh, her pottery more beautiful
and strong than any in the village.
Her family works in the fields all day
and she feeds them as best she can.
She has come to be known as a hard woman.*

f

Five

But she keeps the children always
in her mind: one daughter will be
married to the son of a clan leader
and the other to a priest. She has told
her daughters the story of the three
sad sisters who must lean upon one another.
Her daughters will accept the husbands
she has chosen for them. For the three
strong sons she will do even better.
She prays to the moon and the river.
Let hunters pray to the sun,
she knows where power is for a woman.
Her children will not be field hands
all their lives, where the land gives
fewer ears of corn each year
and the rain seldom comes. Others
will labor in the fields for them.

She watches her daughters for the signs,
and when the time is right, she sends
each one to the path beside the river
and tells her to gather arrowweeds
and wait for a particular young man.
When he passes, she should laugh at him
as if in scorn, and taunt him. Later
she should let him touch her breasts
and offer him her turquoise shell.

g

For her sons she makes more difficult
arrangements with the heads of other clans,
matters which involve much bargaining
over precious amounts of corn.
She tells her sons to bring home
no shells of virginity, whatever happens
on the path by the river. They will
be given more valuable shells later
by the daughters of clan leaders.
They obey her. What else can they do
with such a mother, whose voice is low
as summer thunder far away
and listened to by everybody?

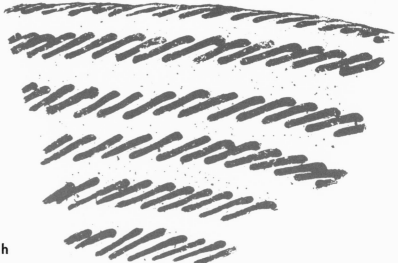

h

Six

Through it all she has no certainty
but she trusts her gods—the river
and the moon, both inconstant. The river
goes dry for seasons at a time
and the moon waxes and wanes
but she prays to both of them,
even in their absence. It seems
to her that they respond. She thinks
she must be doing the right things.

She knows the fields are dying;
each year they give less corn.
Where she once filled five large pots
as tall as her waist at every harvest,
she now fills less than three.
The sun withers the young corn,
which has had little spring rain.
Deer and rabbits are scarce.
There are too many people to feed
and there is something the people need
which the food they have does not provide.

i

Her neighbors have begun to eat
clamshells from the trash heap.
Some eat mice and toads whole
and alive. Some grind up bones.
She knows they are slowly starving
and rations her precious corn
a grain at a time. The ball court
is always empty now, and the crematorium
always in use. But her children
are highly placed. They have more food
than most. She thinks it is good
she prays to the moon and the river
and did what she could for the children.
Perhaps they will survive the drought.

i

Seven

Her husband coughs and becomes thinner
each day, although she gives him
more food than she allows herself.
Twice he has fallen while working
in the field and lay still a long time.
There is some spirit of sickness in him
the priests cannot drive away.
She works in the fields beside him,
often making him stop to rest
under a palo verde. The herbs
she prepares for him have no effect.
She suspects witchcraft but can find
no evidence of it. She prays harder
to her gods, the moon and the river.

Again the hunters return with nothing.
Her husband is too weak to go
to the fields. The air is full of smoke
from the crematorium. He cannot speak.
She sits beside him on the floor,
giving him water, breathing the thick air,
She will not ask her sons for more food;
they have their own children to feed.

The next night, without a word, he dies.
Her sons take him to the crematorium
and perform the necessary sacrifices
for him, but she has no time to mourn.
It is the rainy season. She carries
his tools to the field and channels
water to the stunted corn.

Eight

After the small crop of corn
is harvested, the priests declare
that all who have survived must leave
and find a better place to live.
They say the soil has become the home
of spirits who destroy the corn,
that the rabbits and deer are gone
and the people must make a long journey
toward the path of the winter sun.
There they will find another river,
good soil, many rabbits and deer.

The strong must help the weak.
What they cannot carry on their backs
must be left behind. The gods
will direct them toward a new land
where the spirits will be kind to them.

She takes her place with the strongest
women, her daughters and the wives
of her sons, each leaning against
a leather thong across her forehead
which helps support the burden basket
on her back. The baskets hold corn,
not to be eaten no matter who starves
along the way, but to be planted
at the journey's end. Each guards
her sacred basket. They sleep in turns.
The corn is for the children yet to come.

The march begins at dawn, through the desert
and into the unknown. Behind her
she leaves her husband's ashes,
her river god, her pottery, her home.

k

l

Nine

We do not know if anyone survived
that journey. They simply disappeared
from history or prehistory or whatever
kind of time it was they lived in.
Perhaps they are wandering still
towards the path of the winter sun,
a band of starving Indians, the Hohokam.

They are gone, the River People,
all used up. The river has been
dammed and is dry most of the year,
as if the strong god she prayed to
had followed her away to find a new home.
North of where she lived a great city
has grown up to cover the ruins
of her people. We call it Phoenix,
risen from the ashes others left behind.
But the ruins of her river village
are still there, buried under centuries
of dirt and sand. We pass them
on the freeway and never know
they are less than a mile away,
hidden by time and desert growth.

m

And I can prove to you she did exist.
A team of archaeologists who dug
on the banks of her dead river
found her pottery where she had left it.
Now it lives behind glass in a museum.
I have seen many pass that case
with barely a glance. But sometimes
a woman will stop there and stand
as if hypnotized, staring at forms
the clay took from her hands,
and at the strong geometric patterns
of red on buff with which she painted them.

I remember one. Her voice carried
in the hushed museum. She blurted out
"Oh my God!" then suddenly turned
toward me and I could see fear
in her eyes, a fear of something
she recognized but could not understand.
"What does it mean?" she demanded,
as if I knew and could tell her.
Then she shook her head, involuntarily,
as an animal shakes off water,
and whispered to herself again
and again, "What does it mean?
What in the world does it mean?"

n

o

p

Afterword

The Hohokam were a prehistoric people, remote from us
in time and possessing a culture so different from our own
that even specialists cannot claim to understand it. And yet,
for those of us who live in South Central Arizona, this is a
local poem about local people. We live in their landscape.
We experience the climate and topography they knew.

They were farmers, probably the first farmers in this arid
land, and they survived here, according to the calculations
of experts, for at least 1,500 years—as compared to
European settlement in the Sonoran Desert, which has
lasted about 300 years. They lived along the rivers,
especially the Gila, Salt, Agua Fria, Verde, San Pedro
and Santa Cruz, where they grew corn, beans, squash and
cotton in small plots so intricately terraced to conserve
water that anthropologists have come to call their fields
"waffle gardens." They also built extensive irrigation
systems involving large diversion dams and canals. They
had no domestic animals except the dog, nor did they
understand the principle of the wheel, and yet they
achieved a high culture which produced pottery, jewelry,
and ceramic figures of startling beauty.

Anthropologists are not entirely agreed upon the origins and
chronology of the Hohokam. Some believe that the culture
developed where we find its remains, in what is now South
Central Arizona. Others, among them Dr. Emil W. Haury
whose reputation as an authority on the Hohokam is unsur-
passed, believe they migrated to this area from some un-
known location to the south, in what is now Central Mexico,
well before 300 B.C. and that they arrived with their culture
already developed. Dr. Haury suggests that the most likely
route for them to have taken from Central Mexico would be
up the west coast corridor between the Sierra Madre Occi-
dental and the sea.

There is general agreement, however, that after at least
1500 years of development, during which the population

increased dramatically, the Hohokam culture collapsed rather suddenly about 1450 A.D. Individual communities remained deserted for varying periods of time. Several anthropologists, including Dr. Haury, have made a strong case for the probability that the Pimas (including the Papagos) are descendents of the Hohokam, but this assumption is based upon cultural similarities. There is a gap between the time the Hohokam left their settlements and the Pimas moved into the general area of those settlements.

Many reasons for the disappearance of the Hohokam have been given. Anthropologists feel sure that they were not overrun by a warlike people; there is no evidence of violence connected with their departure. Famine caused by prolonged drought is considered to be a viable reason. It is also possible that after years of irrigation the soil became logged with salts and would no longer grow corn. Another possibility, since the Hohokam probably used no fertilizer to replenish nutrients in the soil, is that the soil simply wore out from constant cultivation.

While all of these reasons might have contributed to the departure of the Hohokam, Dr. Haury feels that none of them is definitive. He does say that evidence based on his excavation and study of Snaketown, probably the largest and longest-lived Hohokam community, indicates that the people living there were protein-starved. The dietary habits of at least some of them, as mentioned in the poem, are not exaggerated. This would point to a lack of game and fish, as well as beans. It is also possible, as we have seen in recent times, that a great increase in population in a limited environment, without an accompanying increase in technology, can lead to famine on a vast scale.

But whatever they were, the reasons for the departure of the Hohokam were broad and cut across cultural and environmental boundaries, since a similar collapse and migration occurred at about the same time among the Anasazi to the north and east, and among the communities

of the *Papagaría* to the south. Could it have been the will
of the gods? We do not know?

My narrative begins in approximately the first decade of
the 1400's, thus making its principal character about fifty
years old at the time of the exodus. The setting is Snaketown
on the Gila River near what is now Sacaton, Arizona.
Thanks to Dr. Haury's painstaking documentation of his
work there, Snaketown is the Hohokam community about
which we know the most; and through his efforts I was
permitted to visit it although it is closed to the public and
guarded. In all physical matters—setting, clothing, tools,
jewelry, etc.—I have tried to be as accurate as possible.
I have seen the pottery, the shell bracelet in the shape of a
snake, the stone hoe. The Hohokam did inlay shells with
turquoise (and even etched intricate intaglio designs on them
with an acid made from the fermented fruit of the saguaro
400 years before etching came into practice in Europe), but
the significance of the shell inlaid with turquoise is my
interpolation.

As for the exodus, perhaps it might not have been as unified
or dramatic as I have portrayed it, but it could have been
in a given community. We do not know if the people drifted
away from Snaketown in small bands or left in the way I
describe, since we know little of their social or religious
structures. We know they cremated their dead, much to
the dismay of contemporary anthropologists. They appear
to have lived in extended family dwellings which, if
modern reconstructions on the Gila River Reservation are
any indication, were dry, commodious, and smelled wonder-
fully of arrowweed, like the inside of a cedar chest.
Because of certain petroglyphs which recur, some anthro-
pologists have surmised the existence of a clan structure.
The idea of priests, I have interpolated; but it is a generally
accepted concept in regard to prehistoric cultures with their
roots in ancient Mexico.

I hope, above all, that the poem is clear and that it might
give the reader some sense of a real person behind an

artifact in an anthropological museum. Beyond that, I have
made no attempt to answer the question with which the
poem concludes. It is a question poets are often asked
about specific poems, and one which they dread. Perhaps
by asking that question of a different form of art, one
whose creator is far removed from us in time and culture,
I can suggest the impossibility of an answer.

Richard Shelton
Tucson, 1985

Richard Shelton has lived in the Sonoran Desert for more
than twenty-five years. Much of the poetry of his twelve
books and chapbooks reflects that desert and its inhabitants.
In 1982–83, under the auspices of the Flandreau Plane-
tarium, Tucson, he wrote and directed a documentary film,
The Sound of Water, which deals with three prehistoric
cultures of the Southwest: Anasazi, Hohokam, and Sinagua.
This poem is, in part, the result of the research done for that
film. Shelton teaches in the Creative Writing Program at
the University of Arizona.

Rebecca Gawa 1985

A letterpress edition of this book was set in 12 point Futura (20th Century) medium italic, with roman, by Mackenzie-Harris, San Francisco. Display types in 20th Century were handset by Charles Alexander and the book has been printed by him on a Vandercook 4T proof press at Chax Press, Tucson, on Mohawk Superfine Ivory. Steven Trubitt photographed the Hohokam pottery sherds at the Arizona State Museum, Tucson—thanks to the Museum and its incredible resources; and special thanks to Mike Jacobs for his ready assistance and enlightened conversation. Steve developed the prints from which the zinc plates were made by the Royal Engraving Company, La Crosse. The silhouette of RS was done by Rebecca Gaver. The binding of the fine edition is by Katherine Kuehn, The Kitchen Binder, Madison. The book was designed by Clint Colby and Charles Alexander. This offset edition has been printed by Fabe Litho and bound by Roswell Bookbinding.